DAVID
CROCKETT
HERO AND LEGEND

bright sky press
HOUSTON, TEXAS

2365 Rice Boulevard, Suite 202,
Houston, Texas 77005

10   9   8   7   6   5   4   3   2   1
Library of Congress Cataloging-in Publication Data

Wade, Mary Dodson.
David Crockett : hero and legend / by Mary Dodson Wade ; illustrated by Don Collins.
p. cm. -- (Texas heroes for young readers ; 7)
Includes bibliographical references and index.
ISBN 978-1-933979-24-3 (hardcover : alk. paper)
1. Crockett, Davy, 1786-1836--Juvenile literature.
2. Pioneers--Tennessee--Biography--Juvenile literature. 3. Legislators--United States--Biography--
Juvenile literature. 4. United States. Congress. House--Biography--Juvenile literature.
I. Collins, Don, ill. II. Title. III. Series.

F436.C95W22 2009
976.4'03092--dc22
[B]   2009007855

Book and cover design by Cregan Design
Illustrations by Don Collins
Printed in China through Asia Pacific Offset

DAVID
CROCKETT
HERO AND LEGEND

MARY DODSON WADE

ILLUSTRATIONS BY

DON COLLINS

bright sky press
HOUSTON, TEXAS

TABLE OF CONTENTS

CHAPTER 1

....

Boyhood Adventures

The short, stubby little boy stood on the river bank in east Tennessee, wailing at the top of his lungs. David Crockett's rosy cheeks turned crimson as he vented his rage. His older brothers had jumped into their father's canoe and left him behind. David's howling protest brought a neighbor. The man quickly saw danger. The current was pulling the boat toward a waterfall. He jumped in and dragged the canoe back to shore.

The Crocketts were living in an area settled by Scots-Irish families like their own. David's grandparents arrived before the American Revolution and quickly joined the push over the mountains. Moving through

Virginia's lower Shenandoah Valley, they finally stopped in North Carolina.

David never knew these grandparents. Like others, they had settled on land that belonged to Creek Indians. The Creek struck back at isolated settlers who had taken over their hunting grounds. The elder Crocketts were killed in a surprise raid. One son was badly wounded and another taken captive, but David's father escaped the attack.

About a year earlier John Crockett had married Rebecca Hawkins. His own cabin was about three miles distant from his parent's home. During this time of fighting for America's independence from Britain, John Crockett shouldered his rife and walked back over the mountains. As one of the "over-mountain men," he took part in the victory at King's Mountain, a battle that helped end of the Revolutionary War.

Soon after returning home, John Crockett moved his growing family to what is now Greene County in east Tennessee. On August 17, 1786, in a cabin at the juncture of Big Limestone Creek and the Nolichucky River, the Crockett's fifth son was born. They named him David, after his grandfather.

Eventually the family included five boys and three

girls. Poor but honest, John Crockett never seemed to get out of debt. He built a grist mill only to have it wash away in a flood. When David was eight, his father built a tavern on the main road between Knoxville, Tennessee, and Abingdon, Virginia.

David helped in the tavern, listening to stories told by hard-bitten wagon drivers who ate and rested there. He was twelve when Jacob Siler stopped at the tavern. The Crocketts had little money. It was customary to hire out half-grown boys for wages. Young David left with Siler to drive cattle to Rockbridge, Virginia.

At the end of the 225-mile journey, he was very homesick. At one place he recognized wagon drivers who had been at his father's tavern and got their promise to take him home. That night, fearing Siler would not let him leave, David crept out of the house at midnight. He walked miles through heavy snow drifts to get to his ride. The heavy wagons moved much too slowly for him. David jumped off and walked the rest of the way.

Both John and Rebecca Crockett had some schooling and knew its value. Although it was a sacrifice, their boys enrolled in the new school when it opened in their neighborhood. Thirteen-year-old David's schooling lasted four days. He got into a fight with a bully. Afraid the teacher would punish him, David didn't go back. Each morning he left with his brothers and returned with them in the evening. They did not tell anyone that he played all day in the woods.

David's father, a man of fearful temper, did not know this until the teacher sent a note asking why the boy was not coming to school. Drunk and angry, John Crockett grabbed a stick and came after his son. David ran. It would be three years before he returned.

David got a job helping a man drive cattle through Virginia. After that 400-mile trip was over, he worked for a farmer, earning 25 cents a day for plowing and planting crops. By the time he was fifteen, David had saved seven dollars.

His next job was with a wagon master hauling goods to Baltimore, Maryland. He was afraid he would lose his money and asked the wagon master to keep it for him.

In Baltimore a new world opened up to the boy. He saw the ocean for the first time. Excitement filled his imagination when a sea captain offered him a job on a sailing ship. The wagon master, however, did not want to lose his helper. He refused to return David's money and threatened to lock him up. Angered by this betrayal, David ran away, leaving his savings behind.

He told the sad tale of his lost money to another wagon master, who vowed to get it back. They found the guilty man, but the money had been spent. Other drivers heard the tale and took up a collection of three dollars. That too was soon gone.

David took a job with a hat maker and worked there for more than a year. The hatter's business failed, and again he was left with no money. The sixteen-year-old decided to go home.

He was not sure how his family would receive him. They might still be angry that he had run away and left them to do all the work. The night he reached home, David slipped into a corner of the tavern but said nothing. He was eating when Betsey, the sister just younger than he, suddenly recognized him. Throwing her arms around his neck, she exclaimed, "Here is my lost brother!" With tears and laughter, the family welcomed him home.

CHAPTER 2

....

Getting a Wife

David was now a stocky, well-muscled young man just under six feet tall, with dark hair, gray eyes, and ruddy cheeks. He felt obligated to help his father pay off some of his debts. After working for six months to clear one of his father's debts, he went to work for a Quaker named John Kennedy.

John Crockett owed money to Kennedy as well. David worked and paid off that debt. Then he borrowed a horse, rode home, and handed his father the paper listing the debt to Kennedy. John Crockett misunderstood. He thought David had been sent to collect the money. The dejected older Crockett told his son he could not pay.

David explained that he had paid it himself.

Having helped his family, David returned to work for the Quaker. He needed new clothes. Kennedy's niece came to visit while he was there, and he fell hopelessly in love. She made his heart "flutter like a duck in a puddle." But she married someone else. "This news was worse to me than war, pestilence, or famine," he said.

Heartbroken, David became convinced that he would have better luck finding a wife if he knew how to read and write. He worked out a deal with Kennedy's schoolteacher son. Four days a week he studied with the teacher. Then, two days he worked on the farm to pay for the lessons and his room and board. He learned basic arithmetic and reading. Soon he could proudly sign his name, putting a line with two big loops under it.

David's second bout with love ended in failure the same as the first, but he succeeded on the third try. He met a pretty Irish girl named Mary Finley at a dance. Everyone called her Polly. To David she looked "sweeter than sugar." Head over heels in love again, he spent the next six months working for Kennedy to pay for a horse.

They were married at Polly's house on August 16, 1806, the day before David turned twenty years old. Her

parents gave them two cows with calves. Kennedy gave them a $15 credit at the store. Polly bought some dishes, and they set up housekeeping. David bragged about how well Polly could spin, weave, and sew. "I have a wife," he said happily. But he had little else.

They rented a farm and worked hard. Son John Wesley was born in 1807, with his brother William arriving two years later. But the Crocketts remained poor.

After five years of unsuccessful farming, Crockett moved his family 150 miles west across the mountains to Franklin County, Tennessee. Land was free. Deer and small game were plentiful. Although he technically was a farmer, David's gun supplied most of their food. He became known as an excellent hunter.

When time came to pay taxes, though, he had no money. They lost the land. The Crocketts packed their meager belongings and joined settlers who were moving farther west. They settled this time in middle Tennessee just north of the Alabama border.

The War of 1812 was in full swing. British troops were fighting Americans. Many of the Indian tribes were angry enough with invading settlers to help the British. Creek Indians killed settlers and burned Fort Mims in southern Alabama. American forces began a bloody retribution. In spite of Polly's pleas, Crockett enlisted to fight. During the diorganized expedition, his hunting skills fed the poorly supplied soldiers.

The war came to a close after General Andrew Jackson of Tennessee crushed the British at the Battle of New Orleans. The victory made Jackson a public hero and later propelled him into the presidency. Crockett was proud to be a citizen of the same state as his hero.

CHAPTER 3

Family Addition

The summer after Crockett got home, his little girl Margaret was born. They called her Polly too. But joy soon turned to sorrow. Baby Polly was only six months old when her mother died.

It was common for a widower with small children to scatter them among relatives, but Crockett did not want to do that. He set out to find a mother for his children, and he didn't have to look far.

Elizabeth Patton owned a nearby farm. Her husband had been killed in the recent Creek War. Elizabeth was an intelligent woman and a good business manager, with $800 of her own money. In addition, her children,

George and Margaret Ann, were about the same age as Crockett's sons, who were now six and eight years old.

Crockett was nearly thirty years old and no longer a lovesick young man. He liked sensible Elizabeth and knew she was a good mother. They were married in 1816 in a small wedding ceremony at her parents' home. Before the preacher could start, however, a squealing pig ran into the room. Amid the laughter, Crockett chased out the noisy intruder.

Crockett had little interest in farming. Elizabeth's well-managed 200-acre farm was ten times larger than his. Still, he wanted to sell all their land and move. The next year, he set out with two companions to scout for a new home farther west.

Soon after the men crossed the Tennessee River, their horses ran away during the night. Crockett traveled 50 miles on foot the next day, trying to catch them. The following day he became ill and was so weak he could not carry his gun. Soon he was drenched in sweat.

He was delirious when friendly Creek Indians found him lying beside the road. Through sign language, they told Crockett he was going to die. They took him to a nearby cabin where his friends found him the next day.

The friends put him on a horse and started home,

but he was too sick to ride far. They stopped at another cabin and left him there. They were sure he was at death's door.

Crockett did not die. He was very ill with malaria, a disease that would reoccur for the rest of his life. It was weeks before he could travel. When he arrived home, his ruddy cheeks were so brown they looked like shoe leather.

Reports had reached Elizabeth that David was dead. Crockett remarked wryly that he knew "that was a whapper of a lie as soon as I heard it."

Several months after he recovered, the Crocketts were on the move again. For the next seventeen years, as they moved westward across Tennessee, Elizabeth was the steady factor in their family. She managed their business while bearing four children between the years 1817 and 1821. Among his "second crop," as Crockett called them, were Robert Patton, Elizabeth Jane, Rebeckah Elvira (Sissy), and Matilda.

CHAPTER 4

....

Colonel Crockett

A year or so into his second marriage, the Crocketts were living in a beautiful area on Shoal Creek in Lawrence County, Tennessee. They built a cabin and settled into a routine as they scratched out a living on the farm. He hunted the plentiful game found in the area.

Before long, Crockett got his first taste of public life. He was elected Justice of the Peace. His cases involved collecting debts and settling ownership disputes. He listened to family disagreements that included a child custody case. From his own boyhood experiences, Crockett had developed a sharp understanding of people. He used common sense and fair play to make his judgments.

Later he bragged that not one of his decisions was ever overruled.

His standing in the community led a man named Matthews to ask Crockett to run as second in command of the militia unit. The militia was an organized group of armed local citizens who protected settlers in the area. Each militia unit elected its own officers. Matthews himself would campaign to become colonel. Crockett agreed to run as his lieutenant. Matthews then invited the whole county to come to a corn husking where the candidates would speak.

When Crockett arrived, he discovered that his opponent would be Matthew's son. He felt that he had been tricked. Matthews apologized and said that his son was very much afraid he would lose to Crockett. Making a characteristic instant decision, Crockett turned the tables. He assured Matthews that his son need not worry. Crockett was not going to run against the young man. He was going to run against his father for the top position of colonel!

The older man, confident he would win, laughed, shook Crockett's hand, and the campaign speeches began. The crowd grew weary as Matthews droned on. When Crockett's turn came, he gave a short explanation. Since he had to run against the whole family anyway, he would just start at the "head of the mess." The crowd roared. He won their votes and became Colonel David Crockett of the 57th Regiment of Militia.

His contagious personality, steady conduct, and sensible decisions made Crockett a respected citizen of the community. He built a gristmill, a distillery, and a gunpowder factory. This used all of Elizabeth's money, and he borrowed more. Although deeply in debt, Crockett finally seemed to have the means to get rid of his money worries.

CHAPTER 5

Lawmaker

With Elizabeth skillfully handling his business operations, Crockett decided to run for the Tennessee legislature. By his own admission, he knew "nothing more about [that] than I did about Latin, and law, and such things as that." His reputation as a solid citizen and his backwoods origins made him a perfect candidate for the people in his area. The problem was that he had to campaign against experienced politicians.

At his first campaign event, he observed that long speeches made people restless. But, when Crockett's turn came, stage fright sucked the words right out of his mind. After a long silence, he explained that he had a speech, but it just wouldn't come out. The audience loved it. He told a few jokes, and he had their votes.

This method of campaigning became his routine. He usually hung back to be the last speaker. When the crowd was tired, he stood up, told jokes and stories, and convinced the crowd he was one of them. The scheme worked. At age thirty-five he was elected state representative for Hickman and Lawrence counties.

When David Crockett arrived in Murfreesboro, capital of Tennessee in 1821, he had already formed the simple goal that governed the rest of his life as a politician. Too many early settlers were being forced to leave their farms. They had settled on open land that the state now took back to give to veterans as a reward for army service. Settlers lost their farms and all the hard work they had put into them. Crockett wanted laws to protect poor settlers from having their land taken away.

Getting elected to the legislature had been easy enough. Crockett lived among backcountry people and understood them. They saw him as one of their own. Working in the legislature was another matter.

He was now in the company of educated men. Their polished speech and manners contrasted sharply with his lack of schooling. Legislators wore the fashion of

the day—pantaloons, waistcoats of the latest style, and ruffles on their shirts. Crockett's pants and shirts were obviously homemade. Even though he did not have expensive things, Crockett never considered himself to be a second-class citizen.

One day a well-to-do legislator referred to him as "a gentleman of the cane." Crockett demanded an apology for this "hillbilly" reference. The legislator passed it off as simply a reference to the place where Crockett lived. Crockett knew better and got the perfect revenge.

He found a man's shirt ruffle on the street and stuffed it into his pocket. When this legislator finished making another speech, Crockett stood up to reply. The ruffle was pinned to the front of his homespun shirt. Laughter burst out, and the embarrassed legislator made a hasty exit. Crockett earned the respect of his colleagues and salvaged his pride. From then on, he proudly referred to himself as "the gentleman from the cane."

He worked in the legislature, confident that his businesses were doing well. Then he got word that a flood had washed away every one of his mills. He hurried home to a devastating situation. All his sources of income were gone, and he faced large debts. Sensible Elizabeth said, "Just pay up…and we will scuffle for more."

Paying debts was an obsession with Crockett. On a trip eastward, he went out of his way to repay a woman one dollar he had borrowed from her husband about ten years earlier. At first she refused to take it, but he insisted. "I owed it, and you have got to take it."

CHAPTER 6

Bear Hunt

After the legislative session was over, Crockett had no money to rebuild the mills. He took teenage son John Wesley with him to scout for land 150 miles west. The 1812 New Madrid earthquake had left the landscape terribly scarred in this part of northwest Tennessee. On the Obion River they found abundant game. Best of all, the land was free and open for settlement.

Crockett chose a site and with the help of his son built a small shelter. They planted a corn crop. Then he went hunting. At the end of the summer they harvested the corn and had enough dried bear and deer meat to supply the coming year.

Crockett returned home and was preparing to move to the new place when the governor called the legislature back into session. He returned to the Tennessee capital. Again, he renewed his effort to keep the state's vacant land open for settlement. It was a law that benefited him and other poor settlers.

Once the session ended, the Crocketts moved to far west Tennessee. Their nearest neighbors were seven miles away. In this hunters' paradise, he filled the larder with venison and wild turkey. By Christmas time, however, he was out of powder for his gun. He needed it for hunting, but he also wanted to be able to shoot guns in the customary way of celebrating the holiday.

Ignoring Elizabeth's pleas, Crockett set off in a snow storm. He was determined to get gunpowder that he had left at his brother-in-law's house. His stubbornness almost cost him his life.

He waded through icy water, holding his gun above his head. He was nearly frozen, but he managed to arrive safely. After four days of rest, he started home. Ice now covered the river, but it was not solid enough to hold his weight. He fell through. He was near collapse when he saw a trail through broken ice. He followed it, thinking a bear had made the opening. Actually, it had been made by the young man Elizabeth had sent to look for him. "When I got home I was'nt quite dead, but mighty nigh it; but I had my powder, and that was what I went for."

That night a bear appeared in his dream. He took it as a sign to go hunting in spite of the ordeal he had suffered the previous day. He began the day by bagging four turkeys. Then his dogs took out after a bear. David followed, but every time he got to the tree where they were baying, there was no bear. This happened several times, and he became extremely angry with the dogs for leading him astray. Then he saw why. Up in a nearby oak tree was a huge bear, the largest he had ever seen. The dogs had been afraid to get any closer.

Crockett's first shot knocked the bear out of the tree. The angry animal started toward him. "I got back in all sorts of a hurry…he would hug me altogether too close for comfort." Three more shots brought the bear down. It took three men and four horses to carry home the meat from the 600-pound bear.

Although his efforts as a farmer brought poor results, his reputation as a hunter grew. He provided food for his family and for neighbors as well. He took wolf skins and bear hides into Jackson to sell. These provided the little real money the family had.

While in town one day to sell hides, he bought some supplies and then stopped at the tavern. Someone suggested that he run for the legislature again, but Crockett said that was not reasonable. He lived forty miles from town. He was too isolated to be useful in the legislature.

To his great surprise two weeks later, a friend came by his house with the Jackson newspaper. An article in the paper stated that he was a candidate. Crockett felt someone was mocking him. He vowed to make them pay. He would run and win!

Using the same crowd-pleasing humor as before, he swayed voters. Again he took his seat in the Tennessee legislature, representing eleven counties in West Tennessee.

By this time he was well-known throughout the state. His objective remained the same. He voted to clear rivers of log jams because these waterways were the main method of travel in his part of the state. When a bill came up to use convict labor to clear the rivers, he objected. He knew that many of these people were in jail simply because they could not pay their debts. He did not think that was fair. David Crockett stubbornly refused to vote for anything he felt was wrong.

CHAPTER 7

Losing and Winning

After serving in the Tennessee legislature several terms, Crockett made a decision to run for the United States Congress. His opponent, a well-known candidate with much more money, won. Crockett smarted over his loss. He left a hired hand to help Elizabeth and set off on a hunting trip.

On the way, he passed a man grubbing tree roots out of the ground to plant crops. He discovered that the man did not even own the field where he was working so hard. Crockett offered him the job of salting and packing the game he shot. By the end of the hunting season, the man had earned enough meat to provide his family with food for a whole year.

One day as he hunted, Crockett followed his dogs as they chased an enormous bear into a narrow, vine-choked ravine. While his dogs barked and baited the animal, Crockett crawled into the tight space and killed the bear with his butcher knife. This bare-handed exploit enhanced his hunting reputation. The huge haul not only provided ample food, it gave him another story to tell.

Still needing cash, Crockett tried a new business venture. He hired men to cut wooden slats for barrel staves. He planned to sell these in New Orleans. The men made 30,000 staves and loaded them on two flat boats. As they left shore, the heavily-loaded boats wobbled so much that they were lashed together. Otherwise, the trip down the Obion River proceeded smoothly. Then they reached the Mississippi River.

The men had no experience with strong currents. They sweated and strained in useless effort to keep the boats near the shore. They were no match for the swift-moving water. They stopped trying to steer and let the river carry them along.

They were near Memphis when Crockett went inside the small cabin to rest. Suddenly there were shouts, followed by a crash. The leading boat had hit a sunken tree

and was going under, pulling the second boat down with it. Crockett, inside the dangerously tilted cabin, could not get out the door. He scrambled to a small window. The crew heard his shouts and pulled him through the tiny opening, leaving his clothes and much of his skin behind. "I was literally skin'd like a rabbit."

Other boats on the river rescued Crockett and his crew from a raft of logs they had managed to reach. But the staves and the money they represented were gone.

Memphis citizens heard about the accident and flocked to the river landing. Wealthy businessman Marcus Winchester was surprised to find Crockett among the rescued men. He took them all to his store. After supplying them with new clothes, he took Crockett home for dinner. Always ready with a story for any audience, Crockett recited the particulars of this adventure and many others, much to the delight of his listeners.

Winchester knew of Crockett and was impressed to meet the man in person. He urged Crockett to run for Congress again. He promised to provide money for the campaign, and Crockett accepted.

The campaign of 1827 election was particularly dirty. Crockett's opponent told lies about him, and Crockett responded by telling even worse lies about the opponent.

Things came to a head at one campaign event. Crockett's opponent brought witnesses to prove that Crockett was not telling the truth. This time Crockett took the stage first. He told such outrageous lies about the man that nobody could have believed them. Then he stopped. Looking at the crowd, he explained that his opponent had called him a liar, and they could certainly see that was true. But, he pointed out, his opponent also told lies. The voters' only choice then was between two liars.

The crowd erupted in laughter. Crockett won the election and was on his way to Washington as Congressman from Tennessee.

CHAPTER 8

....

Go Ahead!

Forty-one-year-old David Crockett arrived in Washington and took rooms at Mary Ball's boarding house. His roommate was a newly elected twenty-one-year-old preacher/lawyer from Kentucky named Thomas Chilton. Despite their different backgrounds, the two became fast friends.

Crockett's goal in the national legislature was the same as it had been in the state legislature—to help the people he represented. Very early in the session he introduced a bill that would make it easy for poor farmers to own land. He would repeat this pattern in every session he served in Congress.

Because he was not familiar with national politics, Crockett expected quick passage. Instead, day after day speakers made endless speeches about their favorite projects, while his bill was ignored. Frustrated, Crockett began to leave early or not show up at all for sessions. He took solace in the taverns where his storytelling and wit put him center stage.

His reputation had spread far beyond his home state. Visitors to Washington were eager to catch a glimpse of this interesting character.

Actor James Hackett became so fascinated that he asked James Kirke Paulding to write a play for him that was based on a Crockett-like character. In the play *The Lion of the West; or, A Trip to Washington,* Hackett played a character named Nimrod, a word that meant "hunter." Hackett began each performance by jumping on the stage wearing buckskin clothing and a wildcat skin cap. He opened the show shouting, "My name is Nimrod Wildfire—half horse, half alligator and a touch of the airthquake—that's got the prettiest sister, fastest horse, and ugliest dog in the District, and can out-run, out-jump, throw down, drag out, and whip any man in all Kaintuck." Audiences ate it up. The play had a successful run in New York and even toured Europe.

By the time the play arrived in Washington in 1833, Crockett was in his third term as a Tennessee congressman. On opening night, he had a special front row seat. Before the performance started, actor Hackett came to the edge of the stage and bowed to him. Crockett rose and returned the courtesy. The audience shouted and whistled approval. This play, as much as anything, burned into the public's mind the image of a backwoods Crockett wearing an animal skin cap.

Long after Crockett's death, Frank Mayo spent twenty-four years playing much the same role in *Davy Crockett, Or, Be Sure You're Right, Then Go Ahead.* The saying, "Go ahead!" became Crockett's well-known motto, and it is possible that he invented the phrase.

The real Crockett, in contrast to the actors, dressed as his colleagues did. Like them, he had portraits painted. The pictures all show him wearing the fashion of the day—black suit, white shirt with high collar, hair slicked down.

After seeing the portrait painted by John Gadsby Chapman, Crockett complained, "It's like all the other painters make of me, a sort of cross between a clean-shirted Member of Congress and a Methodist Preacher. If you catch me on a bear-hunt in a 'harricane,' with hunting tools and gear, and team of dogs, you might make a picture better worth looking at."

Chapman protested that he didn't know how to paint such since he'd never been on a bear hunt and didn't know what a "harricane" looked like. Crockett assured the artist, "We'll make the picture between us, first rate, mind if we don't. So *Go ahead*! Just as soon and as fast as you like."

In preparation for the full-length portrait, Crockett scoured Washington and returned with well worn linsey-woolsey hunting shirt and leggings to his liking. He was very particular about placing the knife on the right and the hatchet on the left. He settled for a rifle that was three inches too short for a Tennessee long rifle, but Crockett selected this one because it had no brass decorations.

The dogs were strays off Washington streets. Chapman wanted to use his own dog, and Crockett relented only after telling the artist to hide the dog's tail. Hunting dogs had bobbed tails to stay out of bear claws.

The artist asked where to put Crockett's name and his motto. "Name on the butcher Knife—Go ahead on the rifle." When Crockett observed that the letters of his name would not all fit on the knife handle, he had a practical solution—just use one *t*. As far as he was concerned, that was enough letters to do the job.

Still, the artist felt the portrait had little life to it. One day Crockett walked in, jerked off his hat, and gave a yell. It was just the right pose. This painting, the only one of Crockett in a hunting outfit that was made during his lifetime, shows the raised arm holding an old floppy felt hat. He was not Nimrod Wildfire. He did not wear a coonskin cap.

The public, however, wanted a backwoods Crockett, and he played to their expectations. Once, a tour group arrived while Chapman was working on the portrait. Crockett lapsed into backwoods speech and action, entertaining them with yarns. When they left, he dropped the act.

Chapman was impressed with Crockett's speech in spite of his lack of education. There was no profanity, and the stories were told with humor and clarity. During the sittings, Crockett expressed his disappointment that editors had changed some spellings and sayings in his autobiography. They wanted the book to sound more like the public expected him to talk.

Matthew St. Clair Clarke had written a highly successful book about him called *Life and Adventures of Colonel David Crockett of West Tennessee*. Crockett was disturbed over inaccuracies in the book. More than that, he needed money. Clarke's book was selling well. He knew he could write a book about himself that would generate much needed cash.

In 1834, with the help of Thomas Chilton, Crockett published his autobiography, *A Narrative of the Life of David Crockett of the State of Tennessee.* On the title page was the verse:

> This rule I leave for others when I'm dead
> Be always sure you're right then, *Go ahead.*

As Crockett expected, the book was a huge success. To provide even more income, he published two almanacs containing yarns and funny stories. In spite of the money that came in, he still was not able to get out of debt.

CHAPTER 9

Frustrated Congressman

When Crockett first went to Congress, he had been a supporter of Andrew Jackson. He believed this president would help the common man. But there was a world of difference between the politician who owned the huge Hermitage plantation and the "man from the cane" who was perpetually in debt.

Crockett was incensed when President Jackson acted to close the national bank that provided loans to poor people. Jackson's plan to remove Cherokee Indians from their homelands brought a rousing condemnation from Crockett. "I believed it was a wicked, unjust measure, and that I should go against it, let the cost to myself be what it might."

Crockett's friends warned him about speaking out against Jackson, but Crockett's sense of honor never changed. He voted for what he believed right and spoke out loudly. He called Jackson "King Andrew" and vowed he would not wear Jackson's collar that said, "My Dog." He paid for his actions by losing the support of Jackson's political party, the Democrats.

The Whigs, an offshoot of the Democrats, opposed Jackson and thought Crockett might be a good candidate for their party. Crockett was well-known, and they knew that he could draw votes. They arranged a lecture tour of the East Coast to see whether Crockett could make a successful run against Jackson.

Leaving Washington while Congress was still meeting, Crockett took a whirlwind tour that drew enthusiastic crowds in New York City and Philadelphia. The Whigs presented him with a beautiful rifle made to his specifications. He called the rifle "Pretty Betsey." It was much fancier than his old "Betsey" hunting rifle. The Whigs soon found, though, that Crockett refused to compromise on anything he thought did not benefit poor people. They withdrew their support.

Then Crockett lost the 1835 election for his seat in Congress. He was almost 50 years old. Everything he had

tried to do to earn money had failed. He sold his farm to his brother-in-law, but he was still in debt. Most disappointing to him and the people in his district, he had not gotten the land bill passed.

Deeply hurt, Crockett headed west again, this time to Texas. He sent a letter to Elizabeth's brother. "I want to explore Texes well before I return."

CHAPTER 10

....

Gone to Texas

With his old hunting rifle in hand, Crockett started out with his young nephew William Patton and two friends. By the time they reached the Red River on the Texas border with Arkansas, he was out of money. That night Crockett's host, Isaac Jones, gave him $30 for his watch.

Crockett stopped at the Swisher home in east Texas and engaged in a shooting contest with young John Swisher. Crockett held forth with his stories late into the night. John Swisher remembered that visit. "He told us a great many anecdotes, many of which were common place and amounted to nothing within themselves, but his inimitable way of telling them would convulse one with laughter."

Two months later Crockett sent an enthusiastic letter home. Writing in January 1836, he told his daughter and son-in-law, "This is the garden spot of the world."

At the time of his arrival, Texas colonists were eager to separate from Mexico. Crockett took an oath to help Texas fight for independence. He joined the Texas army as a private, although he was the acknowledged leader of a group of Tennessee volunteers.

They reached San Antonio early in February, and the arrival of the famous Crockett prompted a fandango celebration. The Texans were caught off guard when General Antonio López de Santa Anna appeared with his army. They scrambled inside the Alamo. Approximately 200 people, Tejano families included, looked out from the old mission at Mexican troops ten times their number.

An angry General Santa Anna ran up a red flag on the church tower, signaling that the Alamo defenders would die if they did not surrender. The Texans answered with a cannon shot.

For days, Mexican cannon blasted away at the Alamo. Crockett and his men took a position on an earth mound behind the picket fence near the mission chapel. Their

long rifles, far superior to the Mexican muskets, found any target in range. But they could not hold out alone, and no army arrived to help them.

Before daylight on March 6, 1836, Mexican soldiers attacked the walls. Twice the defenders drove the attackers back, but at dawn Mexican soldiers poured over the broken north wall. Many defenders died in the courtyard. The rest fought fiercely from nearby rooms. Mexican soldiers broke down doors. A handful of captured men were brought to General Santa Anna, who ordered their execution.

After the battle was over, bodies of the slain defenders were burned. Six weeks later, Texans yelling "Remember the Alamo!" slaughtered Mexican troops at the Battle of San Jacinto. Their victory made Texas a free nation that would last for ten years, until it joined the United States.

David Crockett and the Alamo will always be remembered together, but he was much more than a tragic hero. He was a great hunter who fascinated people with his entertaining stories. Even when bad things happened, he could turn the incident into a humorous story.

These humorous stories caused other people to make up wild ones. They said "Davy" could hug a bear to death. They said "Davy" rode alligators up Niagara Falls. "Davy" stories were not true.

David Crockett was a real person known for his honesty. His infectious personality made him a legend during his life. His death at the crumbling Alamo mission made him a hero to the world.

TIMELINE

1786	August 17, born in east Tennessee
1798	Drives cattle to Virginia
1799	Fight with bully, runs away from home
1802	Returns home, works to pay of father's debts
1804	Learns to read and write
1806	Marries Polly Finley, farms
1807	Son John Wesley born
1809	Son William born
1812	Moves to Lincoln County in middle Tennessee
1813	Joins militia to fight Creek Indians
1815	Daughter Margaret (Polly) born; wife dies
1816	Marries Elizabeth; Robert Patton born
1817	Moves to Lawrence County, Tennessee; Justice of Peace
1818	Elected militia colonel; elected to Tennessee legislature; mills destroyed
1819	Daughter Rebeckah Elvira (Sissy) born
1821	Daughter Matilda born
1822	Moves to Gibson County in west Tennessee
1823	Called "Man from the Cane"
1827	Boats with staves sink in Mississippi River; elected U.S. Congressman
1833	Goes to see Lion of the West; or, A Trip to Washington; writes autobiography
1835	Whigs send him on East Coast tour; loses election to Congress; starts to Texas
1836	March 6, dies at Alamo

AUTHOR'S NOTE

There are several portraits of David Crockett. The smaller formal portrait painted by John Chapman was bought by the Daughters of the Republic of Texas in 1906 and hangs in the Alamo.

The full-length hunting scene was bought by the state of Texas, but the painting was destroyed in 1881 when the capitol building burned. A 16-by-24-inch copy is in the Harry Ransom Humanities Research Center on the Austin campus of the University of Texas.

One of Crockett's rifles is at the Alamo, but it is not "Pretty Betsey." No one can say for sure why he called his rifles "Betsey," but that was the name of his sister.

Just how Crockett died is a matter of debate, but bodies of slain Alamo defenders were burned in three separate piles. In 1837, Juan Seguín, military commander in San Antonio, gathered the ashes. Some of the ashes were placed in the marble vault in the foyer of San Fernando church. There is no way to tell whether Crockett's ashes are there.

Isaac Jones returned Crockett's watch to Elizabeth. She later received $24, her husband's pay for service in the Texas Revolution. In 1854, she moved with her younger children to Hood County, Texas, to live on land Crockett received as a veteran. Elizabeth Crockett's grave in Acton is the smallest state park in Texas.

Because he was poor, Crockett pushed Congress for a land bill to protect others like himself, but he was not successful. After his death, his son John Wesley Crockett became a Tennessee Congressman and helped pass America's first Homestead Law.

Thomas Chilton came to Texas in 1851 as pastor of First Baptist Church in Houston. He died three years later and is buried in Montgomery, Texas.

Although Crockett spent only four months in Texas, the state legislature officially designated him a "Texas Treasure."

SOURCES

It is difficult to distinguish fact from fiction when dealing with sources about a person as well-known as David Crockett. Wildly improbably stories are easy to spot, but even people who met him tended to remember what they wanted to remember. For this book, I used Crockett's own story of his life as well as some eyewitness accounts.

Quotations retain their original spellings.

"Here is my..." David Crockett, *A Narrative of the Life of David Crockett of the State of Tennessee*. Edited by James A. Shackford and Stanley J. Folmsbee (Knoxville: The University of Tennessee Press, 1973), 43.

"flutter like..." and rest of paragraph. *Narrative*, 48.

"sweeter than sugar..." *Narrative*, 63.

"I have a wife..." *Narrative*, 67.

"that was a whapper..." *Narrative*, 132. [*Note: This seems to be an example of the editorial change in language that upset Crockett. He probably would have said* "whopper."]

"head of the mess." *Narrative*, 138.

"nothing more about…" *Narrative*, 139.

"Just pay up…" *Narrative*, 132.

"I owed it…" *Narrative*, 132.

"When I got home…" *Narrative*, 160.

"I got back…" *Narrative*, 164.

"I was literally skin'd…" *Narrative*, 159.

"My name is…" James Kirke Paulding, *The Lion of the West*, ed. James Tidwell (Stanford CA 1954).

"it's like all…" John Gadsby Chapman, "Reminiscences of Colonel David Crockett in 1834." (*Galveston News*, Galveston, Texas, January 27, 1895) as printed in *Proceedings of the American Antiquarian Society at the Annual meeting Held in Worchester, October 21, 1959* (Worcester, Mass: The Society, 1960), 165.

"We'll make the picture…" Chapman, 166.

"Name on the…" Chapman, 170.

"I believed it…" *Narrative*, 206.

"I want to explore…" Crockett to George Patton, October 31, 1835, as quoted in William C. Davis, *Three Roads to the Alamo* (New York: HarperCollins Publishers, 1998), 408.

"He told us…" John M. Swisher, *The Swisher Memoirs*, Rena Maverick Green, ed. (Mrs. J. R. Blocker, 1832, printed San Antonio: The Sigmund Press Inc.), 19.

"This is the garden spot…" Crockett to Wiley and Margaret Flowers, January 9, 1836, copy in Asbury Papers, University of Texas, Austin, Texas.

INDEX